I0749530

Advance Praise for *Protection*

"In bed with a lover in Boston, putting a cat to sleep in Chicago, hanging laundry by moonlight in Washington, D.C. I like the way Gregg Shapiro's stanzas—packed with keen observations and physical details—place me solidly in his world. His in-your-face intimacy feels as necessary as it does generous and brave. Protection is a blessedly open and refreshingly "out" book of poems."

—David Trinidad, author of *Plasticville*

"Moving across the country, Gregg Shapiro finds his poetry on the same highway traveled before him by Henry Miller and John Rechy - at the intersection of sex and night, the place where the brakes go out."

—Carol Anshaw, author of *Aquamarine,*
Seven Moves and *Lucky in the Corner*

"The stirring poems in Gregg Shapiro's Protection offer anything but. These poems touch and say what is forbidden, possessing a fragile joy that is all the more treasured because of the speaker's knowledge of loss. Shapiro's voice is both freshly innovative and strikingly mature. Chicago, Boston, and D.C. serve as flawless backdrops for his perceptive insights the complexities of flawed urban love."

—Denise Duhamel, author of *Two and Two,*
Queen For a Day and *Kinky*

"Gregg Shapiro unveils a geographical trifecta--assembling chatty casual poems about places and people in Chicago, Boston, and DC. This masterful combo of heart on the sleeve devotion, snarky humor, and intimate loss, will catch you up--like stumbling across your favorite tunes on a friend's iPod. Coincidence? Joke? Or possible foreplay? Everyday magic and transcendental mysteries abound. Shapiro navigates these possibilities like a spider from Mars."

—Richard Peabody, ed. *Mondo Barbie* and *Gargoyle Magazine*

"Gregg Shapiro's poems pivot on the minute gestures of intimate relationships and the complications they engender. Anchored in fractured cities and mirages, his thoughtful, textured meditations reveal a depth and vulnerability that connect the intellectual with the visceral. We follow the poet as he leads us into a world caught between devastation and awe, 'Drawn by bird calls, unseen/ footsteps, a song on a portable radio./ The possibility of getting lost, /hypnotic.' Intensely moving, these lyrics are attentive to the emotional wisdom within that must be reckoned with. In the end, it is Shapiro's refusal to surrender his fragile susceptibility that makes reading this brilliant debut such a cardinal experience."

—Gerard Wozek, author of *Dervish*
and *Postcards from Heartthrob Town*

"These are bright, hard, tender and shimmering poems, often breathtaking and unpredictable in their effects. In 'The House of Closed Doors,' for example, 'Fixtures rattle as another door slams and the stairs/consider folding up, relocating. Hinges shiver.' Shiver, indeed. That's what these poems do. In "Roosevelt Island," the speaker evokes our own vulnerability in the following lines: ' . . .I whistle because/I am afraid, because I hope someone/ will hear me. Water scrapes the shore. / I find a familiar path, pick up my pace./ Walk as if I belong, as if I've lived/here all my life." Like Emily Dickinson, Shapiro's speaker is the boy whistling past the graveyard, reminding us all of those things we cannot afford to forget."

—Karen Lee Osborne, author of *Carlyle Simpson and Hawkings*
Co-editor, *Reclaiming the Heartland: Lesbian and Gay Voices from the Midwest*

"These magnificent poems: I keep thinking of them as if they are a kind of travelogue, a slide show illuminating aspects of Shapiro's life, his history and geography, his loves, fears, joys, and family, his preoccupations, the places he's called home. Long after having read them, they continue to flicker in my consciousness, calling me back, asking me to experience, once more, what Shapiro's world holds."

—Kathleen Finneran, author of *The Tender Land*

"Winding its way back and forth across three major American metropolises, Gregg Shapiro's Protection sketches a vivid life-map that's both grounded and vertiginous. Like many of his fearless queer contemporaries, Shapiro crafts daringly personal poems that cleave to themes tried and true—familial and sexual fallout, romantic stalemates and redemptions—all while balancing his long-limbed rhythms with subtly surreal turns. Protection is a visceral debut."

—Jason Roush, author of *After Hours* and *Breezeway*

"With equal parts hilarity and anxiety, the poems in Protection celebrate urban life and lust. In Shapiro's world, every experience, large or small, contributes to his ironic fatalism. Whether the narrator listens to his mother swear, talks to an ex-lover, imagines his house burn, or orders Chinese take-out, all actions reveal his inescapable destiny."

—Kim Roberts, editor *Beltway Poetry Quarterly*

"Official wisdom teaches that writing from the personal is a sin. Gregg Shapiro undoes that strategy, and uses this poetry collection to reveal the virtue of the personal much as a painter uses a large canvas to heighten our senses. We see deeply into details and their mutual complication: into humanity or its absence, into circumstance, anxieties, joys, idiosyncracies, and ironies of life. Shapiro as word-painter would be a mature hyper-realist, and so to call Protection "testament" or "observation" would oversimplify. Instead, the author generously renders enough of himself for the reader to get nearly out-of-body. I leave the consequences of this kind of mental transport for readers to discover and relish for themselves. Suffice it to say, however, that I feel I inhabit this book, even though I know it's not about me in particular."

—Kurt Heintz, editor *e-poets.com*

"This book of cities, of relationships with cities and relationships within cities, is a beautiful map to the poet's heart, revealing the eager and edgy soul of a boy in love. Ordinary and exotic bodies seduce and surround us, shaping new poems with every late night cab ride home. Each poem brings us further into a family that forms itself out of sexy magazines, hand cream and unused condoms, where human defences are peeled back just long enough to see the potential horrors and happiness of love, before falling back into bed to sleep it off. Warm, real, and full of longing, Protection is a poetic experience not to be missed."

—cin salach, author of *Looking for a Soft Place to Land*

"Gregg Shapiro's Protection tells its stories with great warmth and a sharp eye for human detail, spiced throughout with Shapiro's salt-of-the-gay-earth humor. It's such a thoroughly entertaining read that you might sometimes feel like you're savoring a well-crafted first novel, or possibly trading erotic war stories over coffee with an old friend. But then Shapiro's sly, sure-footed way with a simile and the restless 4 a.m. soul that inhabits these pages will tug on your sleeve to remind you that what you hold in your hands is pure poetry."

—Dave Awl, author of *What the Sea Means*
and editor of *200 More Neo-Futurist Plays*

"Gregg Shapiro's stunning debut marks the arrival of a new master poet on the scene. His work blows me away."

—Greg Herren, author of *Mardi Gras Mambo*,
Jackson Square Jazz and others

"Gregg Shapiro's poems are revelations that are more than confessional; they are moments in language worth reading and seeing, worth living through and living for."

—Aldo Alvarez, author of *INTERESTING MONSTERS: fictions*

"Gregg Shapiro mines the psychic realms of the subconscious in poems that are luminous evocations of the play in life. The daily is made mythic in a way that is wry and magical all at once."

—Dan Vera, editor of *White Crane*

Protection

Gregg Shapiro

Arlington, Virginia

Published by Gival Press, an imprint of Gival Press, LLC.

For information please write:
Gival Press, LLC, P. O. Box 3812, Arlington, VA 22203.

Website: *www.givalpress.com*
Email: *givalpress@yahoo.com*

First edition ISBN 13: 978-1-928589-41-9
Library of Congress Control Number: 2007935329

Book cover artwork:
Based on "A Pair of Chicken Hawks Collage," 2000 Copyright © 2007 by James Garrett Faulkner.

Format and design by Ken Schellenberg.

Grateful acknowledgement is made to the editors and staff members of the various outlets in which work from *Protection*, sometimes in different versions, previously appeared:

Amethyst – "Hard To Get," "New Year's Eve Eve"; *Bay Windows* – "Looking At The Ceiling"; *Beltway* – "The Fortune Cookie"; *Bloom* – "Still Talking"; *Bluff City* – "The April Fool"; *Bone & Flesh* – "The Men Want To Be With The Men"; *Christopher Street* – "Putting The Cat To Sleep"; *Dominion Review* – "Bending Over Backwards"; *Folio* – "Color Blind In The Emerald City," "Kisses For Cosmo"; *Getting It On: A Condom Anthology* (Soho Press) – "Protection"; *The Grolier Poetry Prize 1985 – Volume Two* – "The Third Degree"; *Hammers* – "What Are You Dreaming?"; *The Illinois Review* – "Roosevelt Island"; *Lip Service* – "Routines"; *Membrane* – "Wide Awake On Halsted Street"; *Mipoesias* – "Another Close Call," "The Jew's Got A Sale on Suitcases"; *Modern Words* – "My Mother Says The F-Word," "Later Than Late," "The Pizza Eaters"; *Mudfish* – "Black Rabbits"; *The Plum Review* – "February," "The Boyfriend From Another Planet"; *Poetic Voices Without Borders* (Gival Press) – "January"; *QRhyme Poetry Review* – "My Next Boyfriend"; *The Quarterly* – "After The Day"; *Rag Mag* – "Roy's"; *South Coast Poetry Journal* – "Night Laundry"; *The Spoon River Poetry Review* – "Half-Moon Behind Clouds"; *This* – "One of Two"; *Widener Review* – "Color Blind In The Emerald City"; *Willow Review* – "Out The Window, 5:44 AM"; and *WordWrights!* – "The Key Theater".

Boundless gratitude to Robert Giron, Emerson College, American University, Bennington College, Blue Mountain Center, Columbia College, School of the Art Institute Chicago, 69 Prince, 4623 Warren, 634 E, Michelle Fire, Jim Faulkner, Nick at Horizon Café, Allison Peters at the Hyde Park Arts Center, my parents, my sister and brother, my entire extended family, Michael Callaghan, Ken Aicher, Allison Nichol, Denise Duhamel, Maureen Seaton, Dan Vera, Richard Peabody and Lucinda Ebersole, Scott Free, Carrie Barnett and Joann Spyker, Tina Daub, Jay Lordan, Taylor Bowlden, Bill Boyer, Sue Landini, Peter Virgilio, Leslie Bennett, Chris Colacino, Anne Joynt, Randy Abber, John Koulias, Richard McCann, Andrew Holleran, David Trinidad, Rudy Kikel, Ina Rubloff, Jesse Crouse, Washington Gay Writers, E Street Writers, NewTown Writers, SoPo Writers, Chicago Free Press, Feast of Fools, Dusty and k.d., and most especially, Kim Roberts and Rick Karlin.

For Rick, who really understands the power of words.

"I stand in front of you
I'll take the force of the blow"
- Massive Attack, "Protection"

Contents

III. Warren Street, Washington

I. Halsted Street, Chicago

Protection

My mother kept a squat, yellow jar of Topaz hand cream,
a couple of dog-eared paperback mysteries, crossword puzzle
magazines and a red mechanical pencil on top of the headboard.
My father kept condoms and some sexy reading material
of his own in the sliding-door compartment of the headboard,
within his reach. I found this stash once, after detecting
the walnut wood door opened a crack. I carefully turned
a page or two of the book with the missing cover, my hands
shiny and slightly sticky, smelling like my mother's, stopping
when I realized I was leaving greasy, scented fingerprints
on the pages. The foil wrapped discs were only a minor
curiosity, like squeaking bedsprings, garter belts and the box
of Kotex on the floor in a corner of the bathroom linen closet.

When Billy, a seductive, blond next-door-neighbor boy,
and I discovered how much better we liked each other, naked
and excited, in his parents' bed, with our TV-hypnotized
brothers oblivious in the next room, I wasn't surprised
to find his father kept condoms in the same place as mine
did. I wondered if this was something they'd been taught
at school, by their fathers, or an older brother. It never
even entered our minds to unwrap the rubber circles, and
fill them with ourselves. Back then, we only needed
protection from gossipy whispers of jealous children,
the fists of bullies, older and younger brothers, and parents.

There was only one man who ever penetrated me. I discovered how to like it, to relax and accept both the stunning pain and the infinite pleasure of it. The rhythm, alternately smooth and jagged, and the icy hot rush of his exaggerated ejaculation. At the time, when word of the mysterious "gay cancer" began to make its way into polite dinner party conversation and small talk, we took precautions recommended by doctors and those in-the-know. We taught ourselves to forget what a mouthful of semen tasted like, how it felt, warm and thick as phlegm going down. We went to sleep caked in each other's cum, the sheets crusty, littered with condom wrappers, the floor a mine-field of used and discarded rubbers.

"I want you to come in my mouth," he says, as he unrolls an extra-thin latex condom over my erection. Well-versed in the limits of self-control, this was a concept I'd all but disregarded, having learned to override orgasms, to come into the air, onto chests and stomachs, thighs, backs and buttocks. He assures me his teeth will never scratch the sheath's surface, performing magic with lips, tongue, saliva and throat. I look at my penis, chalky, safe and somewhat discolored by the rubber, flashing back for a moment, to a time when the only thing a condom prevented was an unwanted pregnancy. Not entirely foolproof, somewhat sinful and sacrilegious. In a dream, we fill thousands of condoms with the helium spirits of the dead and the unborn. Way over our heads, they become clouds, rolling like acrobats, muscled with storms. I come in waves.

My Mother Says The F-Word

At first, it felt like I'd been slapped across the face –
open palmed and swift. It reminded me of how she
would try to break up fights between my brother
and me, in the back seat of the car, while she was
driving. She would take her shoe off the foot that
wasn't needed for braking or accelerating and flail
around behind her on the off chance of making contact
with a flying arm or leg. This would make us laugh
so hard that we soon forgot why we had been fighting.
My father had been saying it for years, the word
coming out as easily as air. I know my mother
must have been dying to try it out for herself, slip

into it like an expensive Italian pump. I know I learned
to say it before I ever heard my father use it at the dinner
table, over the phone, in a traffic jam. He waited until
we were old enough before he spat it at us, watched us
retreat a little, than treat him like one of our schoolyard
buddies. It will take some getting used to, hearing it from
my mother's mouth. A mouth not accustomed to such
expressions or outbursts. A mouth full of praise and
kisses, outlined in Quicksilver Coral lipstick and easing
into the smile of someone who knows they're too old
to have their mouth washed out with a bar of soap.

Insecurity

I.
Lately, my dreams are multi-limbed. Squids
and spiders, centipedes and sixteen wheelers.
I dream of transformation, shapes with multiple
sides. I am running at half-speed, a marathon
of metaphors and metamorphosis.

II.
Trees, sprouting countless branches, aimed
just out of reach, past the sky, scratch at sleep's
open windows. This will end badly and I will
get caught, my fingerprints like germs, on
everything. I will wave a blur of white flags,
hold all my hands high over my head; surrender
defeated, harmless, cornered, blushing plum.

III.
What is the square root of solitude?
I say my multiplication tables aloud,
to myself, positive there is safety
in numbers and repetition. I decide not
to decide. Fate pushing me around
like the neighborhood bully. Where is
my mother, now, when I really need her
help to fight a battle she never even
imagined? She has been with the same
man for more than thirty years. She
is my example and my downfall.

IV.

I revise my revised schedule. One eye
on the clock, the other tugging at the calendar
like hair. Make a date, break a date, anything
but show up late. I am all over the map, tracked
like some vehicle with a built-in homing device.

V.

I am the diaspora; home is anywhere
I take off my clothes. Meet me by
the river, where the bridge salutes
the sky. Even the spies have spies.
Where will I find my next disguise?

Limping Towards Chicago

This is what I'll do: put a bullet through
my foot. Change my hair color in gas station
restrooms along the way. Collect silverware,
coffee cups from diners, truck stops. Grow
a beard, shave it off. Leave long, long sideburns.
Knock out a tooth, darken the rest with black

licorice. Pick up a dialect, roll it around
in my mouth, spit it out like a seed. Lose sight
in one eye, gain it back in the other. Wish on
the first star, the fifth. Leave eleven different
forwarding addresses. This is where I'll go
to lick salt from my wounds. Produce scar

tissue. Confident in my disguise; recognized
by everyone. Accept the key to the city,
call me the Village Idiot. Try strangling myself
with the phone cord. My father unwinds it,
massages the creases from my throat. Crawl
through thumbtacks I planted in the carpet.

My mother plucks them from my knees and
palms, applies Mercurochrome and gauze.
At least my brother and sister aren't surprised.
They're shaking their heads, selling tickets.
I shrug like a city with big shoulders. The sun
is so bright in the morning, I could sleep four years.

Becoming My Mother

1.
First, I notice it in my voice. In the words
I hurl carelessly, viciously at you. Lethal,
jagged shards where cut crystal and cobalt
glass should be. My tongue, split and forked,
bent and twisted like the knees of a cypress.
It will take years of cautious chewing, swallowing
back to return it to its tasty, lip-licking, French
kissing origins. I will monitor volume and hiss,
curl and response, syntax, sneer and sensation.
Practice throwing my voice like a ventriloquist's
echo, a boomerang, a life preserver.

2.
Suddenly, there are dead or dying animals
everywhere. Random pigeon and seagull
carcasses strewn across the lanes of Lake Shore
Drive. Flattened squirrels and injured rabbits
on display like bizarre museum pieces. Limping
stray dogs and cats with mouth tumors. So, when
I notice the mourning dove, eyelids fluttering, breathing
as slow as an early July breeze on the roof of the blue
Honda, I try to imagine what my mother would do
in this situation. Would she scoop it up in freshly
manicured and lotioned hands? Nourish it through
an eye-dropper? Coo to it, coddle and nurse it back
to full flight health? I shove my own nail-bitten hands
deep into my pockets, past the keys, coins and cash,

until my fingertips strain the seams, knowing there is
nothing that I can do. I think about how you would
laugh at this, shaking your head the way my father
did when my mother would arrive home with
the latest in a series of injured creatures in her arms,
knowing that there is another side to us. One we display
when we think no one is looking, paying attention.

Out The Window, 5:44 AM

What are you supposed to see when you look out the window after the loudest scare-you-awake-noise you have ever heard? A big, humming sound that rattles walls, windows and cuts off electricity. That's right, alarm clocks, air conditioners and VCRs, radios, answering machines. A fat, vibrating sound that you feel in your skin, that reminds you of outer space and martians, unfriendly aliens, extra-terrestrials landing on the roof of your house. So loud it makes the dog whimper and the cat howl like a big baby. Are you supposed to see about ten old men in hunting gear pushing shopping carts down your street? Yeah, your street in the middle of the city. Try to explain that formation of lady cops on motorcycles, smoking cigars. Don't get me started on the dead birds scattered across the lawns and doorways of your neighbors' houses. You can be sure I don't want to talk about the orange and white winged spiders crawling all over the art-gum eraser on the table. Or the electric company truck, turning the corner on two wheels, speeding the wrong way down your "Do Not Enter", one-way street.

New Year's Eve Eve

When I wake up at 4:45 AM to take a pee,
his side of the bed is empty. The sheets,
cold and smooth as the patches of ice
on the street. He is not at his desk

in the office off the kitchen, one hand
moving rapidly over the computer keyboard
while he lights a cigarette from the butt
of another. He is not asleep on the couch

in the living room, light from the television
painting his skin in constantly shifting hues
and patterns. He is not walking the dog.
Her day-glo pink leash is hanging on the hook

by the front door. The note on the kitchen
table says he is buying a gallon of skim milk
and a pack of cigarettes at the 24-hour Jewel,
less than half a mile away, and he has been gone

for hours. Back in bed, I consider making a list
of things to celebrate. The end of one year,
the beginning of the next. The blue moon I must
remember to observe. I do this so as not to think

of where he is, where he might be. In a hospital
emergency room after a car crash or a sudden heart
attack at the supermarket or the 7-11. Slumped
over the steering wheel at a deserted intersection.

Maybe he's in a bar full of other men struggling
to stay warm and lucid. In someone else's bed,
finally putting the handcuffs and rope to good
use. I am stalling for time, for his return,

for the chance to invent an explanation for his
absence. Wondering, as the numbers on the clock
turn to question marks, what I will tell his family,
his best friend, dying slowly and painfully, without

a fight, in the guest bedroom. That his guardian,
his caretaker isn't coming back. The only one
he can trust to ease him through the transition
from old year to new, from this life to the next.

January

Over time, winter in Chicago loses its Arctic edge,
the principle of frigid surprise. Predicted snow
blanketing equally, remaining holiday frills, cars
parked haphazardly along the curb, shingles, pavement,
drain pipes and pedestrians. The snowflakes, liberal
and without prejudice, as diverse as the residents
in this sunlight deprived, weather-beaten neighborhood.

A few weeks into the official winter season, closure and
rebirth, linked permanently together. By the sixth day
of the new year, it's already taking its toll, famous
strangers' names clogging the obituaries. Amidst
the flurry of tardy gift exchanging and tree dismantling,
there is passing mention of appointment book refills
and resolutions. An ex-lover calls with belated holiday
wishes and to tell me that he's found a new boyfriend.

I know I should tell him how happy I am for him,
but all I feel is dizzy, divested of aura and speech.
Is it a sudden change in the air pressure or fear of being
replaced, abandoned, forgotten? Expensively dressed
television weather-forecasters notorious for their displays
of smug boredom, bordering on amusement, and wizardry
with blue screens, issue warnings in pinched

"I told you so" tones. There is a proper way to shovel heavy, just-fallen snow, to apply the brakes when a car starts to skid, to cure depression brought on by the grey veil of winter. At the end of a day-long storm, there are shimmering street lamps and headlights, shy fingers of lightning scratching the sky, and luminescent snow cover.

White, and its variations, corrupted by tire tracks and exhaust, footprints and animal urine. The blue glow of late afternoon, lingering and insistent, the color of hope. The guarantee of the thaw, the season of longer days and abundant light just beyond the horizon, out of the steadily declining temperatures' greedy reach.

The Mid-April Fool

I opened the window. I opened my mouth
but nothing came out. Not a sound but
the sound of the street lamps hissing, "go
back to sleep." He was already gone, he
was halfway down the block, underground,
in the garage. He was starting the car,
putting on miles. I put on his bathrobe,

licked clean his ashtray. I walked the dog
up the back stairs to the rooftop. I howled
at the moon, I danced like Nijinsky. Closer
to the edge I chanted his name, a wakeful
lullaby. Give me a chance, give me a hint.
If I can borrow a dollar maybe I can buy
an umbrella or a clue, a reason for staying.

Later Than Late

Night ticks off silently – a pulse within a pulse, naming
the minutes. Ignoring the clock won't make it go away.
Waning moon, covered by a flap of dark sky. Serrated edge
of dawn, pleats the pitch above the lake. There is something
funny about staying up past your bedtime. The limits we set,

allowances we make for more or less. Bargains struck like bells
in a clock tower. The next day's light moves in like a lover.
Even airplanes in the distance overhead, easily confused
with falling stars and shifting planets, sound different, as if
the air, too, was thick with sleep. Someone needs to be on that

red-eye to somewhere. Blankets of jet lag, recirculated oxygen.
Destinations uncertain as dreams. The ringing in your ears
continues, pure and crooked. An alarm clock, abandoned
phone booth, jackhammer. Movement into dark places
as the night fights to stay afloat above your head. Figures

pair off, form an uneven paper-doll line or jagged circle.
Counting is a convenient method of keeping your eyelids
from staying shut too long, inviting sleep. How many
major intersections from here to there? The length of
a song. The money in your pocket. The phone numbers
of the dead, the living, the disconnected.

Wide Awake On Halsted Street

This is not a dream. This is me, sitting
in the back seat of a cab, 4:30 AM stinking
from sex. The flags are flapping and my teeth
are chattering and I can still taste him on my
lips and gums. I don't hail just any cab, I wait

for one of those new ones that look like whales
on wheels. I want to start a conversation with
the cabdriver, certain he's caught a whiff of me,
leaving something behind on his new upholstery.
But I'm afraid of what my voice might sound

like; shaky and whispered. So, I watch his
pine-tree shaped, peach-scented air freshener
dangle and twirl from the rear view mirror.
I contemplate the comfort factor of the wooden
beaded contraption on his seat. I consider

betrayal and the pleasures of lubrication. I know
if I asked him what time the sun was due to
rise, he would tell me. I know if I asked for
advice, he would lean over the seat to comfort
and console me, like a bartender. I give him

a big tip for a small fare and ride the elevator
I got stuck in this morning and fall into bed,
fully dressed. The sheets will smell like me
and someone else. The alarm won't wake me.
The sun will rise and I will be fast asleep.

Half-Moon Behind Clouds

for Ken

1.
When the dust settles and the smoke clears, I'll be here
or maybe I won't. I'll be nursing my wounds, secretly
admiring them. Imagining the pink, the jagged snap
of scar. Steps going down or a twister, permanent
cloud formations on my skin. I find your fingerprints
all over me, in the strangest places. Where did you
learn to do that? My bed never sang like that before,
never even hummed. It doesn't matter whose on top,
our bodies speak many languages. Fluent, proficient,
no translation necessary. We never have to put on
clothes if we don't want to. So, I won't be tenant
of the year! This is just as good as going door-to-door,
borrowing a cup of sugar, introducing you to my neighbors.

2.
There isn't a natural fiber to be found in this scratchy
blue blanket or this astro-turf-green suburban grass.
Do you think they know, these barefoot and stoned
teenagers, clutching their free concert tickets and roach
clips, what we did last night or this morning? Can they
read it in our eyes, our bodies? I want to kiss you the way
they kiss, without fear or remorse, the way we kissed in
the car on the road. The adjacent sky is humming with
neon and fluorescent flashes, sunset in competition
with manufactured illumination. Are we the only ones
who notice the moon, the broken guitar pick in the sky?
The concert hasn't even begun and I already hear music.

My Next Boyfriend

My next boyfriend won't snore. He'll breathe deep
and easy, restfully. Each lung-filling and emptying
breath, silent as a submarine. He won't have mood
swings, a chemical imbalance or hypoglycemia.

He'll be at ease, as free with expressing himself
as a guy in a Madonna video. My next boyfriend
won't have car trouble or a past. No skeletons, no
closets, no silent brooding moments of inner wrestling.

He won't chew ice cubes, have any addictions or vices.
He won't be tattooed or pierced, scarred or in search
of himself through god. My next boyfriend will arrive
at the dock, a dreamboat, the sturdiest vessel in troubled
waters. My next boyfriend won't be my last.

Putting The Cat To Sleep

I never liked the cat John and Allan named Meeper,
after a pet name they used to call each other
when they were a couple. John kept the cat after
they broke up, moved into separate living quarters.
She was his cat through and through, growling

and hissing, swatting clawless paws at anyone
she perceived as a threat, an invader, competition
for John's attention and affection. We shared John
in the same way Israelis and Palestinians share
their volatile homeland. Grudgingly, suspicious,

always ready for war. Eyeing each other with
malice and distrust for eleven years. John and I
got a dog for balance, to round out our lopsided
family. In the back of my mind, I was convinced
that the presence of another water and food bowl

next to hers would do the cat in for sure. She turned
out to be remarkably ductile for a fourteen year old
feline with a bad attitude. When Allan got too sick
to care for himself, he moved in with John and me.
The apartment reeked of cigarette smoke and cat

urine. In her old age, Meeper had become feeble,
missing the litter box completely, wobbling unsteadily
on her bony legs. We'd go through countless bottles
of Lysol cleanser and rolls of paper towel wiping
up the cat's accidents. The smell overwhelmed

Allan, his lungs still feeling the after effects of PCP.
In a less than democratic fashion it was decided
that Meeper be taken to the vet on Devon Avenue
to be put to sleep. In the sneaky way that coincidence
has of showing up, unexpected, unannounced,

unforgivable, it reared its well-meaning head
that evening. The veterinarian was the same one
John and Allan had taken Meeper to as a kitten
for her shots, when she was neutered, when she
ran a fever from an internal infection, so high, she

panted, her tiny, pink emery board of a tongue
drooping from her mouth. The same waiting room
with separate seating for dog and cat owners, that
medicinally sweet odor, whimpers of animals
in examining rooms. John stays with Meeper

when the doctor administers the shot. I can see
him through the rectangular window in the door.
Allan paces outside of the closed door, occasionally
stopping to chew on a fingernail, glance sideways
into the room. I pull Kleenex from a jacket pocket,

not so much surprised as I am confused at the tears.
Allan opens the door, pets the cat lying still, breathless
on the metal table. I see John's hand, then Allan's, then
a blur. When John turns around to come back into
the reception area, his nose is red and he wipes it

with the back of his hand. I offer him a tissue, but
he is intent on finishing the business of the moment.
Writing a check, blinking back tears. He is amazed
at the speed of the procedure, the precision. "Better
to go fast, then to linger," the girl behind the desk

says, unaware of who else might hear her words.
I look at Allan to see if he has heard. He is staring off
into space, remembering the cat who used to like to
lick his nipples, nip at them when she was just a kitten.
Back in the car, eyes watery and stinging, they are

talking about dinner, as if eating were the next logical
step, some sort of natural reflex or instinct. I concentrate
on driving through the late rush hour traffic. Honking
horns and voices shouting from open car windows.
John has a taste for biscuits and gravy as we drive

past a fast food chain specializing in Southern fried
chicken. I'm not sure if I'll be able to eat, swallow
past the lump of grief in my throat. None of us really
thinks we could stand the hustle and bustle of
a restaurant and we pull into a grocery store parking

lot. Once inside the crowded supermarket, I am
sure I will have a breakdown in the cat food aisle;
split open like a dropped bag of kitty litter, scramble
in pieces all over the freshly washed tile floor, get
lodged under the base of the well-stocked shelves.

Still Talking

Watch his mouth, the way it anticipates
silence. It is a mouth conversant with
the history of oral sex in the men's rooms
of Greyhound Bus stations. The misshapen
teeth, an offensive color, could tear you

another ear, another ulcer. Why does he
bother to shave? Nothing could possibly
cover that orifice, not sheet metal, redwood
bark, wax paper or steel wool stitching.
If he's told you something once, a borrowed

joke or moral in an authoritative public-speaking
tone of voice, you will probably hear it again
and again, without the slightest embellishment
or pretense of truth. The jokes aren't remotely
funny, though he struggles to tell them without

bursting into uncontrollable giggles, and
the morals are immoral. The sloppy kisses
he sends over the phone to voice-mail victims
are the sound of skin being pulled from a bone,
one layer at a time. Rent-boys line up to

relieve themselves into that quivering oval.
He throws his voice effortlessly, when you
least expect it, and the ventriloquists are
so jealous they refuse to speak without
moving their glossed lips. In photographs,

his mouth looks like a cartoon drawing
of a mouth, a courtroom artist's rendering.
Even when he whispers, his north-side-of-Chicago
accent cancels appetites as far south as East
Peoria. Once, a dentist tried to cut out his

tongue while he was under anesthesia. Never
had the dentist seen anything like it; a tongue
with treads like a steel-belted radial tire.
He still talks when he coughs, heaving words
that sound like "cough, cough, choke, cough,

gag." Please don't ask me to describe what
it sounds like when he eats. I only have
the stomach to tell you about his speaking
voice. The way it sounds when it insults
and condescends, especially when he thinks

he is being complimentary and cajoling.
The way his voice rises to the pitch of
a popular high school cheerleader's squeal,
when he laughs. He has a chin, which wasn't
there the last time I looked, but I remember

seeing it once, jaundiced and greasy with his
saliva. Watch the corners of his mouth, the way
they betray his interest in what you have to say.
Notice the way they are poised for interruption,
how they barely tolerate dialogue.

II. Prince Street, Boston

What Are You Dreaming?

The sheet never covers you. You cover it.
Naked, unashamed, on your back, one knee
bent, breathing short, choked night-breaths.

I never sleep on my back, although the doctor
says I should. I make just enough morning
noise. No competition for the gargantuan
garbage truck, grinding dinosaur-large down

Prince Street. Your morning erection points
a little to the left of your stomach. Sometimes
in the morning when I am dressed for work, I
want to climb back into bed, next to you.

I want to whisper in your ear in the language
of sleep, ask you what his name is. I know
he is smooth, blonde, not coarse and muddy

like me. His muscles are taut, intricate,
curvaceous. He glistens, never sweats.
You smack your lips, roll so as not to
disturb the cat, alternately purring and

hissing at your feet. There is no room
in this bed for me now. I put my shoes
back on, fall down the stairs, knowing nothing
will wake you and it's foolish to even try.

Black Rabbits

Black rabbits hang, feet
bound, split seamed, upside
down in the meat market window.
Jet black fur, shiny black eyes,

dulled by the butcher's blade.
Ears drawn, stiff, listening
to tunnels of white noise
and silent sides of beef.

Kisses for Cosmo

I.
Cigarette smoke is deafening. Invisible needles
in my ears. I can't remember the sign language
alphabet beyond F. You promise to write legibly
on a note pad. I blow kisses through your smoke
rings, dissolve the filters with nail polish
remover. Once in a while I remember what
your voice sounds like. In a café on Hanover
Street. The espresso is too strong. You struggle
to be heard over the shouting Italians.

II.
We took the train to Harvard Square. 99 degrees
and the streets were almost still. I drank
iced tea, taking big gulps that hurt to swallow.
Cosmo smoked clove cigarettes, turned somersaults
in the Cambridge Common. Grass-stained and sweaty,
he kissed me on the mouth, looked around to see
who was watching. "One day," Cosmo said, "I will
eat you alive, never let you out." I just want
to hold his hand, tell his fortune, take his pulse.

III.
He talked about buying a motorcycle or getting
a tattoo. I tried to imagine him missing an arm
or a leg, chasing me around the laundromat
or the clubhouse on crutches. The tattoo said,
"Space Kadet". I find that I am repeating
myself more than usual. He's managed to stay
drunk for six days, but who's counting.

The Jew's Got A Sale On Suitcases

"Guy," Fat Anna bellows from the bottom of the stairs.
"Guy," this time louder. Then his response, muffled
behind the closed apartment door, two flights up, "Yes."
"In the wardrobe," she says, decibel level the same,
"next to the bed, where I keep my shoes." "Your shoes,"

he echoes as he opens the door. "There's a straw purse
with flowers," she's giving detailed instructions slowly,
carefully, "where I keep my money." He's listening,
maybe adjusting his hearing aid. "Money," he repeats
a mynah bird in baggy wash pants and a faded flannel shirt.

"Bring it to me. The Jew's got a sale on suitcases. I want
you to see them." He is shuffling away from the door
into another room. In the vestibule, Fat Anna hums, checks
her watch and her nails, maybe tries to run her fingers
through hair thick with years of lacquer and peroxide.

Sitting on the edge of the bed, more awake than I want
to be at this hour on a Saturday morning, in the apartment
below theirs, feet touching the floor for the first time
today. Now I know where the loot is stashed.

The Third Degree

Everywhere I turn, the house is on fire. Crackling,
ablaze, commanding my attention. First, the kitchen,
the hottest spot, second only to the burning bed.

Silverware burned black, crumbles like crackers.
Dishes bubble and warp, glasses explode like the fourth
of July. The smoke alarm is merely a shadow of ash
on the wall. In the living room, one thousand record

albums disappear in a flash. Thirty years of vinyl
vaporizes in less than thirty seconds. Bookcases
and shelves smolder, flames lick at the bindings

and covers of dog-eared novels. Yellowed pages
grey before age. In the bedroom, the wardrobe
and closets are just so much dust. The mattress
and box spring are gone. All that remains are glowing

red coils. I run into the bathroom, stick my hands
into the toilet, but the water is boiling. Before the mirror
melts, I watch my hair ignite, flicker like a candle.

Looking at the Ceiling

Rug burns on my elbows, tailbone, shoulder
blades, scalp. Burn for burn, I still come
out ahead. Wonder how I can go to the beach,
take off my shirt in public (everyone will
know!). I will lie on my back, basted in
sunblock, naming clouds. For now, I will lie
on the sand-colored carpet, stare at the galaxy

of water spots on the ceiling. Cobwebs
are moonbeams, jutting out from the light
fixture. Your face is a planet orbiting mine,
light years away. Our lips collide, tongues
tangle, teeth clack like a meteor shower.
Satellite hands, you are out of this world.
Tell me again about the big bang theory.

The April Fool

I opened the window I opened
my wrists and let myself drip
onto the rain-damp pavement
three stories below my head
pounded the pillow banged bone
against foam my eyes did somersaults

Mexican jumping bean marbles all
I could hear were feet on stairs
keys in locks zippers I want
to strap myself to a bottle of pills
and swallow the phone when it rings

Bending Over Backwards

Not so much addicted
to the pills as to the idea.
Two every three or four.
One every six. Not to exceed
240 breaths per hour.

Sweating in places I never knew
I could. My hair is so clean, it
squeaks. I slide from the bed.
I can't stop evaporating.

Every whisper is a yell
and the songs sound the same
at every speed. All the sentences
and paragraphs are one long

word. The clock and the calendar
have become my best friends.
The mail is always late. If the doctor
asks me my name, I'm afraid
I won't remember it.

One of Two

I list my options on a matchbook
cover: sleep to forget, sleep
to sleep. Walk the Freedom
Trail. Crawl. Go to South
Station and start over.

The Pizza Eaters

The bored waitress never looks at us as she recites the list of daily specials from memory. Minimal eye contact as she takes our orders, drums a ball point pen on her pad. We already know what we want. The same thing we come here for night after night. Doughy crust baked flaky, golden crisp. Generously doused in tangy, authentically spiced tomato sauce. Layered in abundant handfuls of finely shredded, grated mozzarella, Parmesan and ricotta cheeses. Liberal sprinklings of crushed red pepper, basil and oregano. We are here to take in the whistling hiss of the espresso machine. Breathe the weighted air, cloudy with second-hand smoke and accents, stale, expensive perfumes and body odors. There is music, Tony or Frank or Rosemary Clooney from a jukebox in the bar. The minestrone is the color

of mahogany, diced vegetables floating in the steaming broth. Glass cruets of oil and red wine vinegar precede the house salad, limp flaps of lettuce dangling over the sides of the wooden bowls. Forks and spoons lifted, abandoned, traded for knives. This is the pizza parlor where we chose to say good-bye. Our lips stinging from the blend of seasonings, gums aching, tender from gooey, hot mouthfuls of pizza. In a Chicago-style pizzeria, in a different city altogether, we came together to come apart. I must control my hands, gripping my silverware like close friends. As much as I want to wipe the sauce from the corners of his mouth, with the napkin knotted in my lap, I won't. Instead, I make sure to chew my food until I can swallow it like a sob. If he offers to pick up the check, I just might let him.

III. Warren Street, Washington

Color Blind In The Emerald City

You told me it would be easy to get lost
in a city shaped like a fractured diamond.
North and south are just mirages, complicated
by compasses. I never could refold a map
the right way. Landmarks are helpful if

the weather is cooperative. Since it hasn't
stopped raining, I threaten to stand in the middle
of the street, head back, mouth open, and drown.
All I see is black and white. Words on a page,
swimming before my eyes; something magnified

under a microscope. Tourists have never seen
anything so green. Grass that won't die, trees
that refuse to change colors, shed their leaves.
Didn't you notice that block of burned-out
buildings? Look, that used to be the Bible

History Wax Museum. Now it's another gray
area. See those men warming their hands over
a pile of burning newspaper, smoke the color
of ink. When I told you that you'd need eight
arms to hold me, three heads to watch me,

I never imagined you'd chase me with
a dozen legs down this yellow brick road.

Hard to Get

John, I'm only flirting. Careful not to cross
that fine line where looking back means a pillar
of salt. No regrets, no expectations. No idea
which direction to take, where I might end up.

I spin a bottle, kiss a stranger. Hold a moist
finger up to determine which way the wind
blows. I fast until I'm light enough to be
carried by the current. I address postcards

to you along the way, never find the time
to mail them. In a new city, I don't overstay
my welcome, just linger long enough to not
be arrested for loitering. You would be so

proud of me, getting better at mingling,
making polite conversation. Experience
has taught me when to lower my eyes,
shuffle my feet, when to put my hands

in my pockets, rattle the keys and loose
change. How will you recognize me? I've
changed so much. There are new lines
on my face, some you put there, some time

has erased. I'll leave instructions, clues for you
to find me in a crowded airport bar or a bustling
shopping mall. My eyes are still blue, I'm
still crazy, still watching the sky for a sign.

The Men Want To Be With The Men

My mistake, I guess, trying to convince you
to leave Boston and move to Washington. There
are more men here, I say, eligible bachelors.

Susan shakes her head, violently disagrees.
Disappointment, she says, is a woman's closest
companion. Single women I know are single

because they want to be. I can't hear them crying
into their pillows at night. They aren't the only ones.

Bizzy says the odds are better at Hechinger's Hardware
on Wisconsin Avenue; ten men to every woman.
I wonder how many women know about this or if

there is a network, sworn to secrecy. When word
gets out, they will swarm like bees around the hive,
stinging each other. Once inside, transformed

into spiders spinning webs across the lumber, cable,
tools, nuts and bolts. Salesmen, dazzled by such
a display of beauty, stumble, clumsy as moths.

Backyard

Beetles, big as battleships, cast giant shadows
across the lawn and street, eclipse the sun.
Hover, circle, dive and soar. Swat at them –
their determination knows no end. A neighbor
thinks they have been sent from somewhere in
the Middle East. Outer space, I say, send her
running for cover. Nothing ever happens here.

I am sending postcards from the backyard.
On one, I ask for advice, how to juggle
two lovers without twisting my arm, ending
up in a body cast or traction. On another,
I write, "The weather is fine. Wish you were."

Sprinklers hiss like a chorus of snakes
with lisps. I must remember to look up
the word drought in a dictionary. The mail,
opened and discarded, wilts in the freshly
cut, seeded grass. Cassettes melt in the boom
box as I apply another coat of suntan lotion.
Nothing ever happens here. Nothing.

The House of Closed Doors

In this unpredictable climate, there are two or more
questions for every answer. Birds fly into windows
painted shut, painted the color of a stormless sky.

Paint chips falls from the ceiling, collect on warped
wooden floors in lazy, geometric patterns. Fear beads
like sweat on our upper lips. Dressed in camouflage,
white to calm our unsteady nerves. If we really were

phantoms, these blanched bone walls would do more
than just support, flesh out an undernourished structure.
They would know our deepest secrets, what we mean by

privacy, freedom, blindness. Instead they are witness
to changes out of context, out of our control, outraged.
Fixtures rattle as another door slams and the stairs
consider folding up, relocating. Hinges shiver.

Sisters

There are three girls running
There are three girls running nowhere
Rickie Lee Jones

The house reaches up around us; brick arms,
slate scalp. Words like fortress, convent,
asylum come to mind, engrave themselves
on our tongues. Wind bends trees outside.
Inside our posture is perfect. We might

as well be sisters. Six blue eyes staring,
faces lit up by color TV rays. Change
channels, change the subject by remote
control. We take turns, take a vow
of silence, only talk during commercials.

When one of us coughs, we know it is just
a furball; retrieve a glass of cool water,
administer a gentle pat on the back.
We read books, get better at reading each
other's minds. Congregate in the kitchen

to swap recipes, advice on love, tips on
travel for trips we will never take. Maybe
we will cut, color, curl our hair; polish
our nails, the furniture. In the yard, under
wide-brimmed hats, we do the gardening,
come to terms with weeds as willful as men.

Night Laundry

It must be forty degrees. I can see my breath
as I hang wet clothes on the line. They emit
their own steamy, feathery gasps. The neighbor
lady thinks I'm crazy. She watches from her
kitchen window, chain-smoking. I know she
will bring this up at the next block meeting.

Hands so cold, it is difficult to maneuver
the clothes pins. I shake the clothes out
before hanging them. Sending smoke signals
to the moon. A stray cat watches suspiciously
from a safe corner of the yard. Alley lights
make its eyes glow. While I hum and
hang, the cat appears to frown, nod.

The moon is almost full. Laundry basket,
half-empty. I put on a puppet show with
clothes pins. They converse in a language
close to French. Dew just begins to settle
on the grass. It is past the neighbor lady's
bedtime. I make up a story to help her sleep.
The end is scary enough to give her bad dreams.

Running Out of Language

From the tip of my tongue to the back
of my mouth, words escape me. Elusive,
evasive, exclusive as numbers. Parts
of speech play possum, Scrabble dance.
Vowels threaten to take consonants hostage,

make them silent if their demands aren't
met. Nouns refuse to mingle with verbs.
How can I tell you how much you mean
to me? About the woman upstairs who floats
around her room in a flannel nightgown.

February

The boss's wife comes to me with secrets
I must take to heart, to my grave, beyond.
Spilling from lips, thick with red. Punctuated
by brown eyes darting, silent clicks in code.

Facts to be filed, stored for future reference.
She told me that she broke down in the shower.
Crumpled into a heap of steam, salt and water.
Her dreams keep me awake at night. Vivid dreams

of forbidden addictions, another life. Now I know
why February can be as cruel as April. Twenty-eight
days, mimicked by March, with little or no chance
for improvement. Just the promise of white going
gray, hardening like cement.

Another Close Call

"Her legs are matchsticks –
Her face a death mask"
National Enquirer

1.
Las Vegas hasn't been the same since Joey Heatherton
retired, so Daddy gambles, plays the nickel slots.
Mama stays behind, minds the store. Later, she will
feed the children left at home, study the weather map
in the newspaper. In a photo album on a high shelf in
the coat closet, there are Kodacolor snapshots, past trips
to Vegas, Hawaii, Aruba, Key West. One photograph
in particular of them, standing in a clear blue pool under
green plaster seahorses spouting colorless water. No scars
on her breast yet. His heart, still limber as an acrobat.

2.
It's just me wandering the aisles of the neighborhood
drug-store. Lingering over the gossip rags, fingering
over-the-counter remedies. I am searching for a cure
for something I don't understand. What is the definition
of resistance? I dress in black, cook up acts of rebellion,
wonder if I am too old to cry. I put this distance between
us, consulted an atlas for good measure. Something
I've become professional at, without much training,
practice. I could call collect, but the line is always busy.

Routines

So it's Sunday night and I think about
calling you. Maybe calling you a cab.
We could drive around the block, drop me
off in a strange part of town. I will
find my way back, like a latter-day Hansel.

Sing to myself, off-key, like my father,
wonder if I am my own wicked step-mother.
Back at square one, you shuffle the marked
cards, crack your knuckles. Atlantic City
doesn't know what it's missing. I am missing

in action, resolved to a fate that leaves me
crooked and humble. But it's Sunday night
again. So, I primp, take my place at the bar,
invent confidence. Remember the time you
clucked your tongue, said "creature of habit"?

I was never sure if you were talking about
me or yourself. The bartenders whistled
"Here Comes A Regular," when they saw you
coming. Now I look over my shoulder discover
I am the only one standing there.

The Key Theater

I always wondered if anyone saw me break down, standing
as still as a movie poster, in front of the Key Theater
on Wisconsin Avenue in Georgetown, that Saturday night
in March. It was right after watching "Parting Glances"
with Taylor and Bill. It was right after breaking up
with John for the first time, over the phone, long distance.

I pretended that I had something in my eye, rubbing and
rubbing, my fingers shiny and slightly greasy from tears
and smelling like the fake butter they put on the popcorn
at the concession stand. I pretended that I had a popcorn
kernel stuck in my tooth, my mouth twisted into trying
not to cry. Taylor and Bill were at least half a block

in front of me, talking about the cute guys in the movie.
Cute guys talking about cute guys made my chest hurt
and breathing as hard as learning how to drive stick shift
the night Bizzy was too drunk to pull out of the parking
space across the street of The Zebra Room. It wasn't until
they got to the corner of the block where we had parked

Bill's car, that Taylor and Bill noticed my absence, my
lack of contribution to the chatter, and ran back, like two
amateur athletes who had just completed their second
marathon in record time, to where I stood avoiding a crack
in the sidewalk. They put their arms around me like I
imagined they put their arms around each other, the way

the lovers in "Parting Glances" embraced. We walked to the white Jetta that way, arms hooked over and under and over, as quietly as if we were walking on sand. We walked the way Susan and I did after sitting through all nine hours of "Shoah" at the Key Theater. Susan and I left the theater, soggy, crumpled napkins disintegrating

in our fists, our heads hung so low, our necks hurt later as we compared the impressions our chins left on our chests. Taylor and Bill knew I would talk when I could, and I bet they wondered what I thought of the movie, whether I thought they were as cute as the boys who lived and danced and loved and died in New York City.

The Fortune Cookie

Once, I opened a fortune cookie in a Chinatown
café only to find it empty. A clam with no pearl,
a magician with nothing up his sleeve. I made up
a fortune that went, "Drink from the well of life,
but beware of the algae." The cookie was
as hard to digest as the improvised fortune.

Once, I met a lawyer who seduced me with words; then
his hands. A smooth-skinned, smooth-talker who made
my ears blush, my stomach do flip-flops. He tried me
on the roof of his DuPont Circle high-rise, found me
innocent. The next morning, I opened a fortune cookie
for breakfast. It said, "Lawyers do it in their briefs."

Once, a fortune in a cookie ripped in two, each
tattered half contained in the cookie's folds.
Carefully, I retrieved the two-part fortune, fit
the pieces together like a jigsaw puzzle. Jagged
cookie quarters lay on the table, uneaten. "You have
a split personality," was what the fortune said.

Once, delirious from hunger, I neglected to tip
the ancient man who delivered egg rolls and shrimp
fried rice to the house on Warren Street. The food
was hot, filling; satisfied my craving. I washed it
down with green tea, stored the leftovers. The fortune
cookie was stale, as difficult to open as a vault.
It said, "Don't press your luck."

Roy's

They shoot horse in the window of Roy Rogers'
in Georgetown, don't they? Someone told me
they saw them, poor little rich kids with stiff
mohawks, bleached hair. Now, I'm stranded
in a Roy's somewhere in Virginia, eating French
fries with Ellen. Ellen, on her second cup

of coffee, worries that the windows of her car
in the parking lot, aren't rolled up all the way,
as a storm rages outside. Two tables away,
two men discuss movies. "Godzilla Versus
King Kong" and "The Cowboys" with John
Wayne. "What do I know about cowboys?"

one asks, "I'm from Washington. I only know
about Senators." The other stutters in a drawl,
chain-smokes. Ellen wishes she had a deck
of cards. Wishes she had an umbrella. A man.
She'd settle for a man with a deck of cards,
holding an umbrella. The door opens and

teenage boys with flattops and hickeys, girls
with heavy eye make-up running down their
cheeks come inside for milk shakes, chicken
nuggets. Wet clothes clinging to their bodies
like second skin. I am fidgety, lump in my
throat, as a nicotine fit threatens to make

my hands shake. Sunburned from a weekend
at the beach, I am not thinking straight.
I refuse to ask the amateur film critics if
I can bum a cigarette. I would rather run
through the flooded parking lot to the car
as lightning strikes a telephone pole, sends it
crashing down on me like a hammer and nail.

Roosevelt Island

Planes fly low overhead. We swat
at tiny invisible insects. Unable to
relax, listen to the end-of-summer
air. On a dare, I explore the island

alone. Drawn by bird calls, unseen
footsteps, a song on a portable radio.
The possibility of getting lost,
hypnotic. I have no bread to make

crumbs, no sense of direction, no
matches. My breathing loud, sounds
like speech. A language I have studied,
never grasped. I hum to drown myself

out, to imitate electricity. Twigs, stones,
snap, crackle beneath my feet. Pop
like breakfast cereal. I whistle because
I am afraid, because I hope someone

will hear me. Water scrapes the shore.
I find a familiar path, pick up my pace.
Walk as if I belong, as if I've lived
here all my life.

Security

1. Not one, but two men in the midst of a man
shortage. Friends coil like snakes. Backs arched,
cat-hiss, attack ready. I shrug my shoulders
up to my ears. Whistle "Lucky Guy."

2. Call him Mr. X. The man sleeping alone
in the apartment we shared, 500 miles north
of here. He sends me gifts, photographs,
enticements. A new set of keys. Scented
letters that tick like time-bombs.

3. We never learn from history. I draw a seven
year time line with crayons. Fill in the blanks.
Wear it like armor, a bandage, a belt. Fly
a kite, hang curtains from it, make a tourniquet.

4. There is a man in Baltimore who believes
in God. When I kiss him, his mouth tastes
like flesh and blood. I confess I gave up
on religion long before I stopped eating
red meat. When he comes I know I am saved.

5. Two men to make my heart do cartwheels,
my head spin like a bottle. I forget to breathe
when they're not around. Hands quick as light.
Voices in my ear like a drug, a bug buzzing
in, out, in, out, in.

6. In a crowded P Street bar, at a table full
of sailors, I am finally alone. Wandering
eyes tell all before I open my mouth. Words
would only fail me now. Smoke rolls
overhead, lazy as fog. I pull the strangers
in closer; a blanket, family. Like security.

After the Day

How long did you say
it would take for you
to have a nuclear dream?
Things falling from
the sky, even the sky
itself. Pieces of atmosphere
big enough to trip over.

I call my mother
in Chicago. The phone rings
ten times. Ninety-nine
miles for every ring.
Glass in her hair
blends with the gray.

First, my hair comes out
in strands. Embedded in
my palms, new lifelines
to knot and braid. My mouth
is an open sore. I leave
fingerprints on my scalp.

The Boyfriend From Another Planet

Your hands tell you that his skin is like yours;
warm to the touch, sensitive to pressure.
There is hair on his forearm, short and soft
and curved in the same direction. It is lighter
than the coarse hairs on your arms. Bones and
knuckles and joints under his long fingers, nails
manicured to a male length. You fight to keep
your hands from the top of his head, from parting
the curls to look for antennae or strange markings.
He tastes like you now, only better, synthesized
and processed. He could take it with him, bottle
it and sell it back to you at a discount.

He gives you a different kind of goodnight kiss
after the first date. Something alien, unidentified.
It is shaped like nothing you have ever seen in your
own solar system. You are aroused, but certain that
you will drift like snow into the sleep of infancy,
a fetus, an embryo. The fragile eggshell rest of
peace and safety. When you close your eyes you see
images of fifties, black and white science fiction
movies. When you open them, his eyes are still there,
close enough to lick. Crystalline, yet faintly pastel,
it's a night's work just looking into them.

His car is ordinary. No glowing digital dashboard, no outrageous numbers on the odometer, no rocket boosters necessary for intergalactic travel. Gravity treats you like equals, even though you would swear that, for a few seconds, your feet left the ground. At last, you admit that he is down to earth. With a voice like warm milk and no trace of an accent, he tells you more about himself, revealing nothing unusual or suspicious. Still, you know he is unlike any other man, naked or dressed, that you have ever met. And as he drives away, his taillights like supernovas, you look up into the starry night and wish on every one, dim, blinking, blazing.

Books Available from Gival Press

Poetry

Bones Washed With Wine: Flint Shards from Sussex and Bliss
by Jeff Mann

ISBN 13: 978-1-928589-14-3, $15.00

Includes the 1999 Gival Press Poetry Award winning collection. Jeff Mann is "a poet to treasure both for the wealth of his language and the generosity of his spirit."
— Edward Falco, author of *Acid*

Canciones para sola cuerda / Songs for a Single String
by Jesús Gardea; English translation by Robert L. Giron

ISBN 13: 978-1-928589-09-9, $15.00

Finalist for the 2003 Violet Crown Book Award—Literary Prose & Poetry. Love poems, with echoes of Neruda à la Mexicana, Gardea writes about the primeval quest for the perfect woman.

Dervish by Gerard Wozek

ISBN 13: 978-1-928589-11-2, $15.00

Winner of the 2000 Gival Press Poetry Award / Finalist for the 2002 Violet Crown Book Award—Literary Prose & Poetry. "By jove, these poems shimmer."
—Gerry Gomez Pearlberg, author of *Mr. Bluebird*

The Great Canopy by Paula Goldman

ISBN 13: 1-928589-31-0, $15.00

Winner of the 2004 Gival Press Poetry Award / 2006 Independent Publisher Book Award—Honorable Mention for Poetry

"Under this canopy we experience the physicality of the body through Goldman's wonderfully muscular verse as well the analytics of a mind that tackles the meaning of Orpheus or the notion of desire."
— Richard Jackson, author of *Half Lives*

Let Orpheus Take Your Hand by George Klawitter

ISBN 13: 978-1-928589-16-7, $15.00

Winner of the 2001 Gival Press Poetry Award

A thought provoking work that mixes the spiritual with stealthy desire, with Orpheus leading us out of the pit.

Metamorphosis of the Serpent God by Robert L. Giron

ISBN 13: 978-1-928589-07-5, $12.00

This collection "…embraces the past and the present, ethnic and sexual identity, themes both mythical and personal."

—*The Midwest Book Review*

On the Altar of Greece by Donna J. Gelagotis Lee

ISBN 13: 978-1-92-8589-36-5, $15.00

Winner of the 2005 Gival Press Poetry Award / 2007 Eric Hoffer Book Award: Notable for Art Category

"…*On the Altar of Greece* is like a good travel guide: it transforms reader into visitor and nearly into resident. It takes the visitor to the authentic places that few tourists find, places delightful yet still surprising, safe yet unexpected…."

—by Simmons B. Buntin, editor of *Terrain.org* Blog

On the Tongue by Jeff Mann

ISBN 13: 978-1-928589-35-8, $15.00

"…These poems are …nothing short of extraordinary."

—Trebor Healey, author of *Sweet Son of Pan*

The Nature Sonnets by Jill Williams

ISBN 13: 978-1-928589-10-5, $8.95

An innovative collection of sonnets that speaks to the cycle of nature and life, crafted with wit and clarity. "Refreshing and pleasing."

— Miles David Moore, author of *The Bears of Paris*

The Origin of the Milky Way by Barbara Louise Ungar

ISBN 13: 978-1-928589-39-6, $15.00

Winner of the 2006 Gival Press Poetry Award

"…a fearless, unflinching collection about birth and motherhood, the transformation of bodies. Ungar's poems are honestly brutal, candidly tender. Their primal immediacy and intense intimacy are realized through her dazzling sense of craft. Ungar delivers a wonderful, sensuous, visceral poetry." —Denise Duhamel

Poetic Voices Without Borders edited by Robert L. Giron

ISBN 13: 978-1-928589-30-3, $20.00

2006 Writer's Notes Magazine Book Award—Notable for Art / 2006 Independent Publisher Book Award—Honorable Mention for Anthology

An international anthology of poetry in English, French, and Spanish, including work by Grace Cavalieri, Jewell Gomez, Joy Harjo, Peter Klappert, Jaime Manrique, C.M. Mayo, E. Ethelbert Miller, Richard Peabody, Myra Sklarew and many others.

Poetic Voices Without Borders 2, edited by Robert L. Giron

ISBN 13: 978-1-928589-43-3, $20.00

Featuring poets Grace Cavalieri, Rita Dove, Dana Gioia, Joy Harjo, Peter Klappert, Philip Levine, Gloria Vando, and many other fine poets in English, French, and Spanish.

Prosody in England and Elsewhere: A Comparative Approach by Leonardo Malcovati

ISBN 13: 978-1-928589-26-6, $20.00

The perfect tool for the poet but written for a non-specialist audience.

Protection by Gregg Shapiro

ISBN 13: 978-1-928589-41-9, $15.00

"Gregg Shapiro's stunning debut marks the arrival of a new master poet on the scene. His work blows me away."
—Greg Herren, author of *Mardi Gras Mambo*

Songs for the Spirit by Robert L. Giron

ISBN 13: 978-1-928589-0802, $16.95

A psalter for the reader who is not religious but who is spiritually inclined. "This is an extraordinary book."
—John Shelby Spong

Sweet to Burn by Beverly Burch

ISBN 13: 978-1-928589-23-5, $15.00

Winner of the 2004 Lambda Literary Award for Lesbian Poetry
Winner of the 2003 Gival Press Poetry Award — "Novelistic in scope, but packing the emotional intensity of lyric poetry..."
— Eloise Klein Healy, author of *Passing*

Tickets to a Closing Play by Janet I. Buck

ISBN 13: 978-1-928589-25-9, $15.00

Winner of the 2002 Gival Press Poetry Award

"...this rich and vibrant collection of poetry [is] not only serious and insightful, but a sheer delight to read."—Jane Butkin Roth, editor of *We Used to Be Wives: Divorce Unveiled Through Poetry*

Where a Poet Ought Not / Où c'qui faut pas by G. Tod Slone

(in English and French)

ISBN 13: 978-1-928589-42-6, $15.00

Poems inspired by French poets Léo Ferré and François Villon and the Québec poet Raymond Lévesque in what Slone characterizes as a need to speak up. "In other words, a poet should speak the truth as he sees it and fight his damnedest to overcome all the forces encouraging not to."

For a list of poetry published by Gival Press, please visit: *www.givalpress.com.*

Books available via Ingram, the Internet, and other outlets.

Or Write:

Gival Press, LLC
PO Box 3812
Arlington, VA 22203
703.351.0079

www.ingramcontent.com/pod-product-compliance
Lightning Source LLC
LaVergne TN
LVHW050940080826
845145LV00004B/1346